C000178933

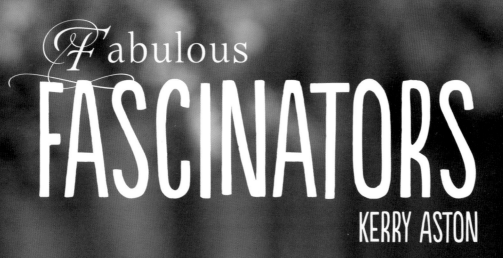

Fabulous FASCINATORS

KERRY ASTON

HOW2HATS
make hats, turn heads

www.how2hats.com

MB MORSE-BROWN PUBLISHING

First published in 2012.
This edition published 2013.

Morse-Brown Publishing
www.morsebrownpublishing.co.uk

Text copyright © 2013 Kerry Aston
www.kjmillinery.co.uk

Studio shots copyright © 2013 Donna Harrison-Smith
Design and layout copyright © 2013 Morse-Brown Design Limited

All rights reserved. No part of this book may be reproduced, stored in a retrieval system or transmitted in any form or by any means, electronic, mechanical, photocopying, recording or otherwise, without the prior written permission of the publisher.

Series Editor: John Morse-Brown
Photography: John Morse-Brown and Nigel Walk
Location photography: Ioana Zamfir (www.ioanaphotography.co.uk) and John Morse-Brown
Shot on location at Selly Manor Museum, Bournville, Birmingham, UK

Design & Production: Morse-Brown Design Limited
www.morsebrowndesign.co.uk

For more titles in this series see www.how2hats.com

ISBN: 978-1-907615-15-3

Notice of Liability. The information in this book is distributed on an "as is" basis, without warranty. Whilst every precaution has been taken in the preparation of this book, the author Kerry Aston, How2hats, Morse-Brown Publishing, their employees or associates, shall not have any liability to any person or entity with respect to liability, loss, or damage caused or alleged to be caused directly or indirectly by the instructions contained in this book or by the products described herein.

REVIEWS FOR FABULOUS FASCINATORS

66 *Truly an amazing and fun book, packed with substance and detail. An addictive manual for hat making hobbyists.* Mandy Kingsbury. **Fashion Director & Stylist. Judge, Jaguar Style Stakes, Dubai World Cup**

66 *What a wonderful, clear and concise book on Fascinators! Not only an inspirational book but also a great reference book for any milliner. It will be a great addition to my library.* Louise Green. **Three times winner of Millinery Designer of the year, owner of one of the most successful high-end millinery companies in the US**

66 *A wonderful, enjoyable book for anyone learning to make fascinators. All the basic millinery techniques are covered. Kerry has created a lovely book packed with information for any budding milliner.* Davina Lynch. **Award-winning Irish milliner**

66 *This is a lovely book to get you started and excited with fascinator making. Easy to follow steps and a variety of ideas accompany each project.* Judy Bentinck. **Judy trained with Rose Cory, Royal Warrant Holder and world-renowned teacher** .

Contents

WELCOME TO THE WONDERFUL WORLD OF FASCINATORS!

Kerry wearing her Florentina fascinator (see page 44).

My love for fascinators first began with a visit, many years ago, to Royal Ascot in the UK. The array of fabulous, intricate and wonderful hats and fascinators was so tempting, I just had to learn how to create my own. So I decided to start by taking it up as a hobby.

From day one I was hooked – after just two lessons I had created my very first fascinator (that's how easy fascinators can be!) But if you had told me back then that I would become an award-winning milliner with my fascinators featured in Vogue, showcased on the catwalk and worn at Royal Ascot, and set up my own successful business, K J Millinery, I'd have said you were out of your mind!

Fascinators have never been more popular, and this book is a wonderful introduction to their creation. Once you've mastered the simple basic techniques, you can go on to create your own unique style – the range you can make is almost infinite and only limited by your imagination.

I hope you enjoy this book as much as I've enjoyed writing it.

Kerry x.

Introduction

This book is a comprehensive introduction to the wonderful art of making fascinators – and fascinators have never been more popular than they are today. It's a book where you can start from scratch with no previous experience, and also go on to make more advanced head pieces with a definite 'wow factor', once you've mastered the simple basic techniques.

Making fascinators is not about hard and fast rules – the secret behind their creation is a handful of quite simple techniques, and finding new ways to use these techniques to create head pieces that are totally unique to you. So I've started by explaining some of these basic techniques – skills that you'll use again and again if you really get in to making fascinators (and I defy anyone not to – it's such an addictive process!)

Making fascinators is also a great way to get your creative juices flowing. Instead of buying specialist tools, with a bit of 'out of the box' thinking you may find there are things you already have about your house that you can use instead. You'd be amazed at what I've made some of my fascinators on – wooden salad bowls and kitchen saucepans have parallel lives in my household!

For each of the 14 projects, I've listed the tools and materials you'll need, and I then take you step-by-step through the making process, with accompanying photos. I'd recommend reading through all the steps before you embark on a project – it's always easier if you start with a clear picture in your mind of what you're going to be doing for the next couple of hours. At the end of each project I usually show a handful of other similar fascinators that can be made by just tweaking some of the methods, sizes and embellishments to give a fascinator with a very different feel.

Enjoy!

> Making fascinators is not about hard and fast rules – the secret behind their creation is a handful of quite simple techniques, and then finding new ways to develop these techniques to create fascinators that are totally unique to you.

A short history of the fascinator

Women have been wearing things in their hair since time immemorial. I bet even cave-women adorned their hair with flowers to catch their hunter men-folk.

In the 17th century, there was a fashion for courtiers to wear really large powdered wigs. The bigger your wig, the more important you were – a bit like houses or cars today. And it became trendy to 'accessorise' these already massive hairdos with some pretty random things – like whole stuffed birds and even complex scale models of sailing ships. We could probably say that these were the first fascinators, although they weren't called that then.

A Woman in Blue (Portrait of the Duchess of Beaufort) by Thomas Gainsborough. 1780

Prince William and Kate Middleton visit Trearddur Bay RNLI Lifeboat Station, 2011. © Getty Images

The term 'fascinator' is pretty recent. When the word was first used in the 1860s, it referred to something like a small scarf or shawl worn over a woman's head. And I suppose from there, they just got more and more elaborate and eventually evolved into the creations we see at weddings and at races today.

The Queen and other members of the British Royal Family have worn fascinators for many years, particularly at Royal weddings. The Duchess of Cambridge (pictured left) continues to wear them and it is she who is partly credited with the ever increasing trend for them.

The great thing about fascinators is that they are *still* evolving. Nothing about them is set in stone, and armed with this book, you can go on to create your own unique look. Happy making!

Design and inspiration

Design and inspiration is all about personal taste and preference. Inspiration can come from many sources: nature, art, food, architecture, seasons and emotions. Anything and everything that is around you can help to inspire your designs. I personally take inspiration from my family, my daughter and visual memories such as a stained glass window, a stunning cloud formation or apple blossom in spring. That is the beauty of millinery – the simplest of objects can inspire the most fabulous creations.

In order to create my fascinators I use many things I already have available at home. Everyday household items such as wooden fruit bowls and even saucepans can be used to create different blocked shapes. I started off crafting fascinator flowers with a fish knife and a melon ball cutter, and used mugs as fascinator base templates. There is almost no limit to what you can use to make fascinators. For embellishments, I collect old jewellery and beads from vintage and charity thrift stores to include in my designs. These all add to the character and individuality of the pieces.

I often start a fascinator with a very clear idea in mind as to how I want it to look... and end up with something completely different! It can be far more interesting to 'go with the flow' and adapt your original idea, so that the piece evolves naturally, rather than trying to stick rigidly to the original idea.

When starting a new project, I usually gather together a collection of materials – the fabric, feathers and embellishments. I then experiment with the various elements in my hand to see how they best work together – and then check how it looks on my head in the mirror.

Your own style will develop over time. There will be some techniques within this book that you'll love, and others that you probably won't, but once you know the basics you can start to challenge yourself and experiment with your own designs, materials and fabrics. After all, your fascinators should be an expression of yourself, a chance to push the boundaries and really have fun with this beautiful craft.

Tools & equipment

One of the great things about making fascinators is that you don't need to spend a large amount of money before you get started. All you will need are a few basic tools, many of which you may already have. I have listed most of these below, and explained a bit about the materials you'll be using for the fascinator projects in this book.

TOOLS AND EQUIPMENT

Fabric scissors. Steer clear of expensive fabric scissors, as cutting sinamay really blunts them. A basic pair will do.

Paper scissors. It may sound extravagant, but I always use separate scissors for paper as I want to keep them sharp.

Darning or millinery needles. A good selection – you'll use (and perhaps lose!) lots of these.

Good quality thread in various colours. If you're going to invest in anything in millinery, spend it on good quality thread and fabrics. Cheap thread will snap.

Invisible thread. Useful for when you really don't want to see that stitching...

Glass head pins. Available from most craft stores.

Tape measure.

Ruler.

Dressmaker's chalk.

Pencil.

Cling film (Saran Wrap in the USA).

Rubber gloves.

Measuring jug.

Wooden spoon.

Masking tape.

Card or paper. Ideal for templates that can be kept for next time.

Glue. I tend to use UHU.

Wire cutters.

Sponge. For applying sinamay stiffener.

Iron and ironing board. If you can, use an old iron that you're not going to use to iron your clothes. Sometimes the dye and/or the sinamay stiffener comes off on to the iron, and this would ruin your clothes if you subsequently ironed them with the same iron.

MATERIALS, SUPPLIES AND SPECIALIST EQUIPMENT

Sinamay. Sinamay is a millinery fabric made from banana fibres. It molds easily and is great for creating different shapes. It comes in a wide array of colours but also dyes easily, so you can dye it to exactly the colour you want.

Sinamay fabric stiffener. You can buy this diluted or undiluted. As the name suggests, it's used to stiffen sinamay so it holds it's shape – when blocking for example.

Petersham ribbon. Also known as cross-grain ribbon. It is used for trimming and edging.

Silk flowers. You can make these yourself or buy them from craft shops.

Various feathers. There's a huge range of feathers – I talk about specific types in individual projects.

Acid dyes. The dyes that I like to use are Jacquard Acid Dyes. They come in powder form, and can be easily mixed with very hot water to dye a large amount of feathers or just a few. They come in an assortment of colours, but buying just a few basic colours and mixing them will give you plenty of shades and hues. Other makes and types of acid dyes are also available, so please do use whatever you prefer.

White vinegar. This is available from any household shop.

Pearl beads. You can get both faux beads and fresh water beads, which are the real thing. The later are more expensive but, in my opinion, worth it.

Clear plastic combs. These are used for attaching fascinators to your hair and can be purchased from craft shops and millinery suppliers.

Millinery wire. Millinery wire is easily manipulated and holds it's shape once bent. It is usually covered and is available in black or white.

Spring wire. This is steel wire and is harder to bend than millinery wire. Great for when you need to hold a shape.

Craft wire. This is for making mounts and you can buy it in packs. It comes in straight lengths and is a bit thicker than millinery wire.

Floral tape. This is specialist tape that, when pulled, becomes tacky. As the name suggests, it is used in floristry. It can be purchased from most craft shops and comes in various colours.

Metal and fabric-covered hair bands.

Millinery elastic. This holds fascinators onto the head instead of hair bands or combs. Usually available in black or white (but can be dyed).

Hat blocks. For this book, a hat block is only required for Mirabella (page 76) and you may find something around the house that will work instead of a hat block. Having said that, making the more advanced fascinators is a great opportunity to acquire some of the more specialist hat making equipment like hat blocks. They may look expensive, but if you treat them well, they will last a lifetime, and it will really boost your fascinator-making opportunities if you can build up a nice little collection. Guy Morse-Brown (www. hatblocks.co.uk) makes beautiful wooden hat blocks.

Blocking pins. You can buy specialist hat block blocking pins, although you may find that drawing pins will do, as long as they're the sort that are easy to pull out. But beware – drawing pins will eventually go rusty and may stain the sinamay.

Mannequin head. I purchased polystyrene ones from eBay, but for really nice ones that can also be used to display your fascinators on, try www.hatblocks.co.uk

$\mathscr{B}$asic techniques

There are a number of techniques that you will use over and over again when making fascinators – making bias strip, making fascinator bases and dying feathers. I've included the instructions for each of these here at the beginning of the book, and I refer to them later on as we need them.

BASIC TECHNIQUE NO. 1
THE BIAS STRIP

Bias strip is used a lot when making fascinators. It can be used for edging, as bases and for trimming (you can make bows and swirls out of it for example). If you know the colours you'll be working with, you can make it up in advance if you prefer. Always keep off-cuts of bias strip, even tiny bits, as you can use them when attaching hair bands and combs.

You will need: one metre of sinamay; a tape measure; fabric scissors; a pencil or dressmaking chalk (optional); iron and ironing board.

1 Lay the sinamay flat on your table or floor. Take one corner and fold it across to the opposite straight edge to create a big triangle. Push the fold down all the way along with your hand, to create a nice crease line.

2 Open the fabric back out and cut along the creased line you've just created.

3 Decide how wide you want your bias strip to be. If it's for a fascinator base, it will depend on the size of the base you are making. A 2 inch (5 cm) strip is good for small 3 inch (7.5 cm) diameter fascinator bases, and a 3 inch (7.5 cm) strip is good for larger 5 inch (12.5 cm) diameter and wider bases. Here we are making a 3 inch (7.5 cm) wide strip. Fold over the cut edge by 3 inches (7.5 cm). You can measure and mark this in advance with a pencil or dressmaking chalk but there's no need really – just measure and fold as you go along. Crease the fold, open it out and cut along it.

4 On your ironing board, fold this strip in half, all the way along the length, and crease it with your fingers. Iron the crease flat. When you're ironing sinamay, just press the iron on for a couple of seconds and lift it off again, repeating as you go along. Don't iron sinamay as you would clothes as this will stretch it. Sinamay also burns really easily – another reason not to hold the iron down for too long.

5 Open the strip back up and fold in each edge almost to the centre, ensuring you leave a few millimetres gap between the edge of the sinamay and the centre fold. If you don't leave a little gap here, the sharp edges of the sinamay will poke through the folded edge of the finished bias strip, and you're very likely to cut your fingers when you're using it later on. Now fold the two folded edges back up again so you have a strip of sinamay about ¾ inch (2 cm) wide, made of four layers.

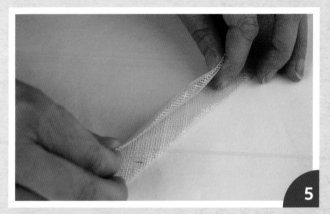

You can now leave it as it is, or if you want, you can make it thinner and longer. To do this, hold one end firmly with one hand, and with the other hand pull the strip towards you. You'll notice that as it stretches in length, the width shrinks. (If you hadn't left a gap between the edge of the sinamay and the centre fold when you were making the bias strip, you'd probably be cutting your fingers on the sharp edges at this stage.) You now have a piece of bias binding twice as long as you started out with.

6 For the final iron, lay the strip on the ironing board pointing away from you, and place the iron gently across it. Carefully pull the strip under the iron, making sure it doesn't linger too long, otherwise it'll burn.

BASIC TECHNIQUE NO. 2
THE FASCINATOR BASE

You will need: sinamay – left-overs will be fine for most bases; spring wire; wire cutters; a template of the right size or something circular to draw round (see templates on page 89); floral tape or masking tape; bias strip of a sufficient length to go round the circumference of your template plus a little extra; fabric scissors; a mannequin head; sinamay stiffener; glass head pins; blocking pins; cling film (Saran wrap in the USA); a sponge.

Fascinator bases can be whatever size you like. For this example, we're making a small one with a diameter of 4 inches (10 cm) suitable for Easy Project No. 1, Marcelle (page 16).

1 Fold your sinamay in half to create two layers. Pin your template through both layers of sinamay. Carefully cut out the circle shape. You now have two identical circles of sinamay.

2 You now need to wire the edges of the sinamay so that it will hold it's shape. Measure out a length of spring wire to fit round the circumference of the circle, and cut it with about ½ an inch (1 cm) extra with which to bind the ends together. Start to secure the overlapped ends together with either floral or masking tape, but before you finish securing them, double check the diameter is correct. If it's not, adjust it so that the wire circle is the same diameter as the sinamay circles, and then finish binding the ends together tightly.

3 Attach the wire to the two sinamay discs using a blanket stitch, stitching at about ½ inch (1 cm) intervals all the way round the sinamay discs. Don't sew too near the edge of the sinamay otherwise the thread is likely to pull loose – I tend to work about ¼ inch (5 mm) in from the edge.

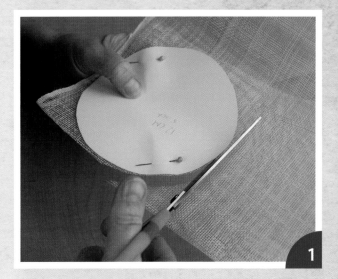

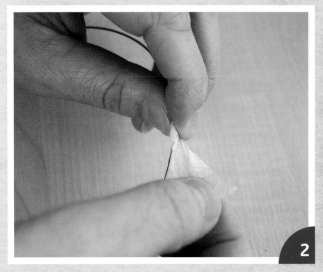

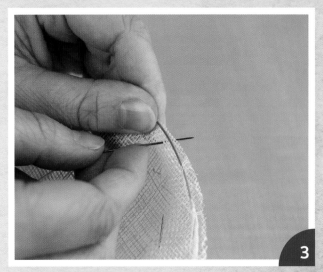

4 Once the wire is secured, the raw edge of the sinamay needs covering with a bias strip (see Basic Techniques No. 1 on page 6 for how to make a bias strip). Take your bias strip and trim the frayed end off one end by cutting diagonally across the strip. Open the bias strip up, and starting ½ to 1 inch (1 to 2 cm) in from the end, place it over the edge of the sinamay and wire disc. Start securing the bias strip all around the disc with a stab stitch (a stab stitch is where you put your needle in diagonally through the sinamay and out the other side, then over one weave of sinamay and diagonally though again, zigzagging all the way round). Mould the strip with your fingers as you go, so that it bends neatly round the edge of the sinamay and wire disc.

5 As you approach the end, bend the sticking-out end of the bias strip where you started from, out of the way, and cut the other end to fit neatly under it. Carry on stitching until you get to the end of the bias strip, and then fold the other end back down on top.

6 Sew down the overlapped fabric securely to give a lovely neat finish.

Depending on the size of your fascinator base, that may be all you need to do. However, if you want to create a curve in the base to match the natural curve of your head, follow the next few steps.

7 Take your mannequin head and cover it in cling film (Saran wrap in the USA). Soak the fascinator base in water by running it under the hot water tap or by placing it in a bowl of hot water. Then place the wet fascinator base on to the mannequin where you want it to be, and securely pin it down all round, using glass head pins or blocking pins (or drawing pins – although make sure they're the sort you can easily pull out again).

8 Dab some sinamay stiffener (mixed one part stiffener to four parts water if you are using non-diluted stiffener) all over the fascinator base with a sponge. Leave it to dry completely before removing.

9 You should now have a lovely curved fascinator base moulded to sit snugly on your head.

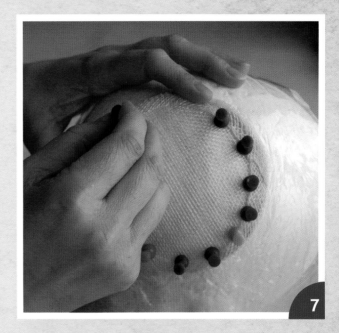

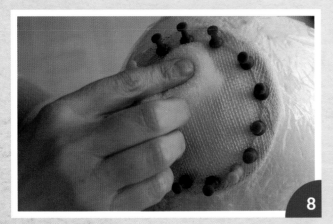

BASIC TECHNIQUE NO. 3 FEATHER DYEING

You will need: Feathers; acid dyes (see my note about dyes on page 5); household white vinegar (I have even used malt vinegar before if I've run out); 2 plastic tubs or baking trays (you won't be able to use them for food afterwards though); paper towels; metal spoon (or wooden spatulas from a coffee shop); boiling water; cold water; rubber gloves.

• Don't clean the feathers before you dye them – feathers have natural oils in them, and if you remove this oil entirely, the feathers will lose their shape and look dull and lifeless.

• If the feather is going to take the dye, it needs to be kept in the dye long enough for the dye to break through the oil barrier.

• The intensity of the colour you get depends on how much dye you put in the water, not necessarily on how long or short you keep the feather in the dye.

• Start with a weaker solution of dye in water, and gradually increase the amount of dye to make the feathers a darker shade. You can always add more but you can't take it away.

1 Put your rubber gloves on. Pur about ½ cup of boiling hot water into one of your plastic tubs or trays. Add about 1/8th teaspoon of powdered Jacquard Acid Dye. Stir the mixture with a wooden spatula or metal spoon. Allow to cool. As soon as it is at room temperature, the dye mixture is ready to use. Place the feathers in, making sure they are all covered.

Swish the feathers around for a few minutes with your spoon or spatula to help the dye break through the oil and penetrate the feather.

2 Fill your second plastic tub or tray about half full of cool water and add two tablespoons of white vinegar. Remove the feathers from the dye and place them in the cool water and vinegar mix. Rinse them around. If at this stage it looks like the dye hasn't taken very well, pop the feathers back in the dye mixture for a bit longer, and then back in the cool water and vinegar mix.

Place paper towels on a baking tray and lay the feathers onto them. Don't worry if your feathers all look out of shape and shrunken – you haven't ruined them! Leave them to dry at room temperature. If they still look a bit bedraggled when they're dry, just gently fluff them up with your fingers.

It is worth pointing out that dyed feathers are not water-resistant. The dye will run in the rain, so take an umbrella if there's a chance of rain when you're wearing a fascinator.

Easy projects

The projects in this section are the perfect introduction to the wonderful world of fascinators. They can be worn on any occasion, and are not too complicated to make. They can also all be easily adapted to fit your own style.

My five easy projects can all be completed in a relatively short space of time – anything from thirty minutes to an hour and a half. You'll find with fascinators that the more you make, the faster you become.

These easy projects are also an ideal way to practise the three basic techniques that you will have learnt in the first section. Once you've mastered them, you will be ready to start experimenting with your own designs.

WORKING WITH VEILING
EASY PROJECT NO. 1: MARCELLE

Approx 1 hour   Skill level Easy

You will need: A 1 yard (1 m) length of 12 inch (30 cm) wide veiling; 1 x 4 inch (10 cm) fascinator base; 2 turkey arrow quills; fabric scissors; needle and matching thread; hair comb.

Prepare two needles and double threads.

1 Start by pleating the veiling. This is really easy – just lay the veiling on your work surface, and starting from the cut edge (i.e. one of the 12 inch (30 cm) wide edges), fold the veiling over about 1 inch (2.5 cm). Now fold it back on itself by the same amount, and then just continue doing this, alternating the folds like you would to make a fan, pinching and gathering with your fingers. Keep going until all of the fabric has been gathered up.

2 Pick up the folded strip of veiling and hold it securely in the centre.

3 Taking one of your prepared needles and double threads, wrap it around the centre of the veiling a couple of times where you're holding it and tie it off in a knot so it's really secure. You'll notice that when you let go of the veiling, it 'pings' out into a circle. Leave the needle and thread hanging, and place the veiling to one side.

4 Take your fascinator base and arrange the two turkey arrow quills on it, crossing them over each other in the centre. Secure the first feather by sewing through the fascinator base and through the side of the feather spine. You may need to sew through the spine in a couple of places close to each other, to make sure that it's securely fastened on to the fascinator base.

5 Place the second feather on top and secure it in the same way. Give it all a good shake to make sure they're both securely attached.

6 Take your veiling with the needle and thread that you left hanging and, placing it on top of the feathers and fascinator base, push the needle down through the fascinator base in the centre, between the two feathers. Stitch through a couple of times to make it all really secure. Tie off the thread underneath the fascinator base and cut off any excess.

7 Before you attach the comb, experiment in front of a mirror to see where you'd like the fascinator to sit on your head. Once you have decided, you'll know where to attach the comb.

8 Now take your hair comb and stitch it on to the back of the fascinator base, wrapping the thread around the comb and a couple of the teeth at each end.

Congratulations! You've made your first fascinator. Now to wear it and wait for the question: *'what a gorgeous fascinator – where did you get it from?'*

As with all the projects in this book, once you've learnt the basic techniques you can start to experiment. That's what making fascinators is all about – it's not about hard and fast rules – it's about learning a handful of simple techniques and then looking for inspiration and new ideas. I've included a couple of ideas to get you started on the opposite page.

Marcelle

Leonora

Gina

Anais

Ideas to steal

Try sewing pearls and crystals onto the veiling (Leonora), or using different feathers or flowers (Gina). Experiment with 9 inch (23 cm) veiling instead of 12 inch (30 cm) veiling for a more compact fascinator.

MOULDING BIAS STRIP
EASY PROJECT NO. 2: CERYS

Approx 45 minutes   **Skill level** Easy

You will need: 1 yard (1 m) of bias strip; stripped hackle feathers (you can buy these by the yard or metre but you only actually need approx 20 individual feathers); floral or masking tape; glass head pins; needle and matching thread; hair comb.

1 Take a yard (1 m) length of bias strip. Hold one end of the strip between your thumb and forefinger, and with your other hand gently create a loop by folding the strip over onto itself.

2 Holding the centre securely, repeat the process in the opposite direction to create a figure of eight shape.

3 Whilst holding the centre, create another figure of eight. This loop will need to be slightly longer as it will form the centre of the bow. If you are struggling to hold it firmly, pin, then continue.

4 Make a third and final figure of eight – this needs to be the same size as the first figure of eight.

5 You will then have three figure of eight loops. Using your needle and thread, secure the three loops together in the centre. Cut off the excess bias strip in the centre of the loops, where it can be hidden later.

6 & 7 Now gather together a collection of approximately five hackle feathers and secure the ends of the stems together with floral or masking tape. Continue this process until you have enough little bundles of feathers to decorate your fascinator. I have used four but it's entirely up to you how many you would like.

8 Insert one bundle of feathers at a time between the bias strip loops, pushing the stems in as far as possible towards the centre of the bows.

8 Once you are happy with their positioning, sew the feathers to the bias strip by sewing through the centre of the bows. Don't worry if the sewing isn't completely neat – as long as it's close to the centre of the bows, it'll be covered by the loop of bias strip that you'll be wrapping round the centre in the next step.

9 Once all the feathers have been secured, take the excess bias strip that you cut away, and wrap it around the centre of the bows. Secure it at the back by folding the edges underneath to create a neat finish, and then sew it firmly in place.

10 Now take your comb and stitch it to the back of the fascinator, wrapping the thread around the comb and a couple of the teeth at each end.

Congratulations – your second fascinator. Wear with pride! If you would like to experiment further with this technique I have included a few ideas on the opposite page.

6

7

8

9

10

Cerys

Chantal

Ava

Amelie

Cerys is perfect for a cocktail party, a christening or just to jazz up an outfit. It's a really easy fascinator to start with as it doesn't need much in the way of materials, and it's quick – it shouldn't take you longer than 45 minutes.

MOULDING BIAS STRIPS
EASY PROJECT NO. 3: COLETTE

Approx **45 minutes**   Skill level *Easy*

You will need: 1 yard (1 m) of bias strip; 2 pearl stems; 6 coque feathers; 1 yard (1 m) of ¼ inch (5 mm) wide satin ribbon, either in white or a matching colour; glass head pins; needle and matching thread; fabric scissors; floral or masking tape; hair comb.

1 Take your length of bias strip. Gently bend the end round on to itself to form a neat loop.

2 Repeat the process in the opposite direction so you have a figure of eight with two identical loops.

3 Turn the figure of eight over and repeat the process above so that you end up with two figures of eight, back to back, on top of each other.

4 Hold the centre securely with your thumb and finger and pin in place. Sew through the centre of the figure of eight with a needle and thread to hold it all together.

5 Now to 'trim' the fascinator. Take three coque feathers and a pearl stem and place them together. Neatly trim the ends to the length you require using your wire cutters, and secure them together using floral or masking tape. Make two sets of these, one for each end of the figure of eight.

6 Place a set inside the loops at each end of the figure of eight. If you want to be doubly sure they are securely fixed, you might want to dab a spot of glue onto the ends of the feather and wire bundles before you insert them. Then sew through the bias strip loops with a needle and thread so the feather and pearl bundles are securely attached to the sinamay.

1
2
3
4

Make sure you keep the stitching fairly close to the centre of the figure of eight, close enough in for it to be covered by a width of bias strip in the next step.

7 Now take some of the left-over bias strip and wrap it around the centre of the figure of eight, making sure you cover both the join and all of your stitching. Cut off the excess and secure the loop together at the back by sewing it in place.

8, 9, 10 & 11 Now to secure the comb to your fascinator. For this project I have wrapped some white silk ribbon around the spine of the comb and sewn that to the fascinator – it gives it a very nice look. To do this, start by dabbing a spot of glue onto one end of

the spine of the comb, and then, securely holding one end of the ribbon against the glue, begin to wrap the ribbon around the comb's spine and between the teeth. When you get to the end of the comb, cut off the excess ribbon and

glue the loose end down. Stitch the comb to the back of the fascinator with a couple of stitches through the ribbon at each end of the comb's spine.

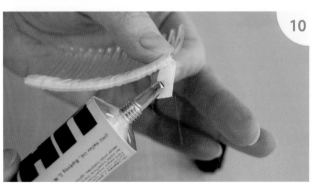

Colette

Mimi

Beatrice

Ideas to steal

Other examples of this technique are Beatrice & Mimi. For Beatrice, I glued ribbon to the loops, and to make Mimi, I glued some crystals onto the fabric to give it a bit of a sparkle.

SINAMAY FLOWERS & PETALS
EASY PROJECT NO. 4: COURTNEY

Approx 1 ½ hours   Skill level Easy

You will need: Approx ½ yard (½ m) sinamay (or off-cuts); paper or card for template; beads to decorate; paper and fabric scissors; pencil; glass head pins; needle and matching thread; 3 inch (7.5 cm) fascinator base; comb or hair band.

1 Photocopy the template on page 89, enlarge it and cut it out. Or just draw a 7 inch (18 cm) diameter semi-circle and cut it out.

2 Lay your sinamay flat and place the template on the sinamay, lining up the straight edge of the template with the bias edge (i.e. diagonally across the weave) and pin it in place. Draw round the template with your pencil.

3 Cut out the sinamay and repeat until you have five sinamay semi-circles.

4 Take one of the semi-circles and lay it on the table with the straight edge closest to you. Fold this edge over about ½ an inch (1 cm) and crease the fold by pressing along it with your fingers.

5 Fold the semi-circle in half, with the folded edge on the inside.

6 Now hold the quarter-circle shape by the rounded edge, with the point facing away from you. Pinch and pleat the rounded edge together with your fingers, gathering it bit by bit. You'll see a petal taking shape.

7 Sew through the pinched ends to secure it. Sew through the side above where your fingers are – you're going to be cutting the end of the petal off to give you a neater finish, and you don't want to cut through the stitching you've just done. Repeat this process for all five sinamay petals.

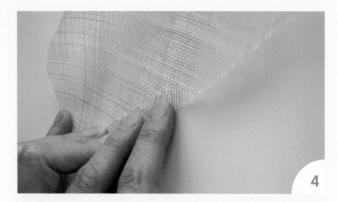

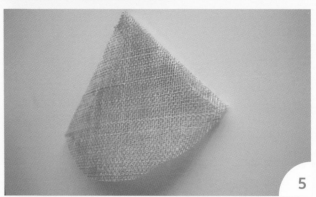

8 Once you have five petals, neaten their edges and cut off any excess fabric so that the petals are all roughly the same length.

9 Take your prepared fascinator base and pin each of the petals in place on the base to create a flower shape. Once you are happy with the shape of your flower, sew all of the petals to the base.

In order to cover the stitches and the joins at the centre of the flower decorate with beads or crystals of your choice. I have used ¼ inch (6 mm) black Swarovski crystals.

Your fascinator is now ready and can be attached to a comb or hair band of your choice. See step 8 on page 17 for instructions for this.

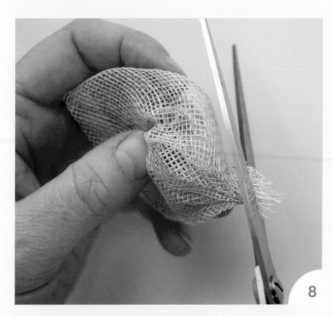

8

9

Courtney

Elouise

Catherine

Elouise is a larger flower with a sinamay bud centre, and Catherine incorporates flowers in the centre of a large fascinator.

SINAMAY & VEILING BOWS
EASY PROJECT NO. 5: NAOMI

Approx 1 hour   Skill level Easy

You will need: Approx ½ yard (½ m) sinamay (or off-cuts); approx ½ yard (½ m) veiling; fabric scissors; needle and matching thread; glass head pins; iron and ironing board; hair band – I've used a satin-covered one; glue (optional).

1 Lay your sinamay flat and measure out a rectangle on the bias (diagonally across the weave) approximately 6 inches (15 cm) wide and 12 inches (30 cm) long. Measure another rectangle on the bias approximately 5 inches (12.5 cm) wide and 9 inches (23 cm) long.

2 Take the bigger rectangle and fold one of the longer edges over by approximately ½ an inch (1 cm), creasing the fold by pressing firmly all the way along with your fingers. Then fold this fold over itself again by another ½ inch (1 cm) – just to give it a neater edge and to stop any of the raw edges poking through. Repeat this on the other long edge so that both edges are folded over twice.

3 Repeat this process with the smaller rectangle.

4 Iron both folds on both pieces to neaten the edges, and to ensure the folds stay in place. Iron on a medium setting, without steam. When ironing sinamay, just press the iron on for a couple of seconds and lift it off again, repeating this as you go along. Remember – don't iron sinamay as you would clothes, as this will stretch it. Sinamay also burns really easily so don't hold the iron down for too long.

5 Now fold both short ends over once and iron them to neaten them up. Repeat with the smaller piece as well.

6 Take the bigger piece, and with the folds facing up, fold the two ends in to the centre so they overlap by about ½ an inch (1 cm).

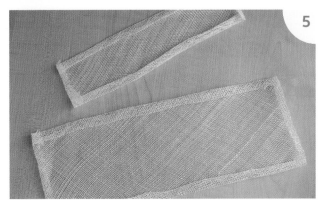

7 Press down and pinch the sides together to form pleats, and you've got your first bow. Taking your needle and matching thread, sew through the centre of the bow to secure it all together. Tie the thread off to stop it coming loose. Repeat this process to make the second bow with the smaller piece.

8 Now place the two bows one on top of the other and sew them securely together.

9 To make the veiling bow, cut a 14 inch (36 cm) length of 9 inch (23 cm) wide veiling. Fold both shorter edges of the veiling into the centre, so the edges overlap by about 1 cm (½ an inch).

10 Now pinch the sides together into the centre to make a bow shape (exactly the same process as you did for the sinamay above). Sew through the centre and wrap the thread around the middle a few times before securely tieing it off. Give it a tug to make sure it's secure and the veiling doesn't ping out.

11 You've now got three bows – two sinamay and one veiling bow. Sew them all together through the centre, with the small sinamay bow on top, the big sinamay bow in the middle and the veiling at the bottom.

12 Before you attach the bows to your hair band, hold the fascinator against the hair band and try it on to see where it needs to be attached. When you have found the right position for it, pin it in place.

13 To finish, take a matching bias strip approximately 1 inch (2.5 cm) wide, and wrap it around the centre of

6

7

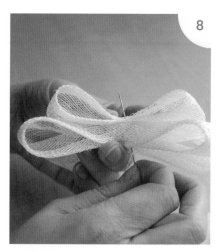
8

9

10

11

the bows and over your satin-covered hair band. This will cover all of your sewing in the middle. Pin the bias strip in place and then stitch through both the satin covered hair band and the bias strip. If you're worried about it not being secure with stitching alone, you can always use a spot of glue, but make sure you sew while the glue is still wet – you will struggle to get the needle through it when it's dry. Cut off any excess bias strip to neaten it up, and you're done!

13

Naomi

This is a good example of a fascinator that can be made from off-cuts. Nothing is wasted in millinery! Great for flower girls or young children. My niece loves this one: *'I love Naomi!'* she says.

Intermediate projects

This section focuses on slightly more difficult but very achievable projects such as creating mounts, rolling edges and working with different fabrics like crin.

These intermediate projects will take you a little longer to complete than the easy ones and will require practice, so don't be too put off if you don't get the desired look straight away. As with any new craft, the more you make, the better you will become. The rolled edge technique for Lily (page 52) is a good example of this. The process requires quite a bit of perseverance, but it's well worth it when you see the finished fascinator taking shape.

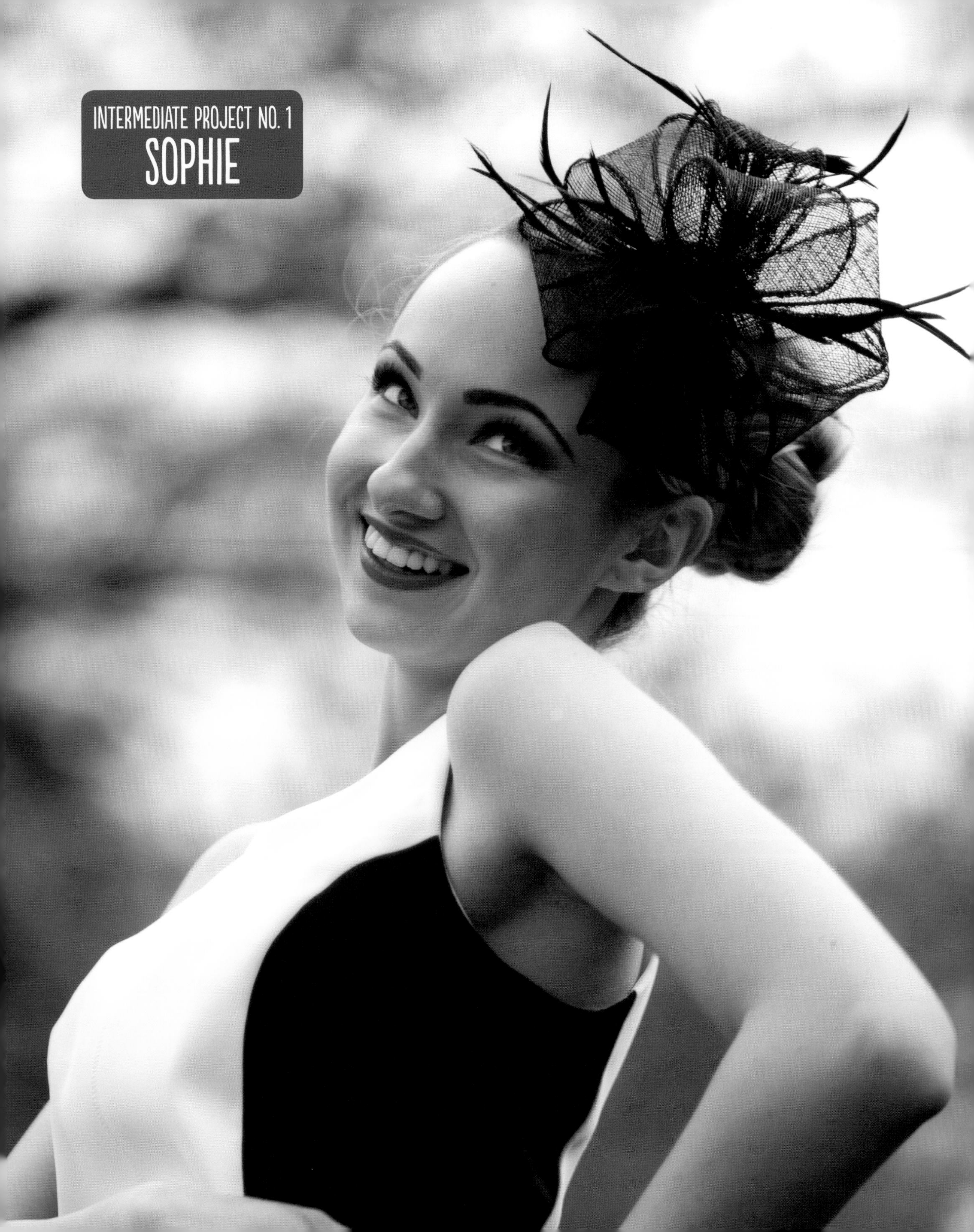

INTERMEDIATE PROJECT NO. 1

SOPHIE

ROLLED EDGES
INTERMEDIATE PROJECT NO. 1: SOPHIE

Approx ½ a day   Skill level Intermediate

You will need: Approx 1 yard (1 m) sinamay (or off-cuts, as long as they're on the bias – i.e. diagonally across the weave); approx 6 inches (15 cm) of goose biot feathers (you can buy these by the metre but some places will sell you smaller quantities); a 3 inch (7.5 cm) fascinator base in matching colour; paper and fabric scissors; needle and matching thread; paper or card for the template; pencil; glass head pins; comb; glue (optional).

1 Photocopy the template on page 89, enlarge it and cut it out. Alternatively, draw a 7 inch (18 cm) diameter semi-circle and cut it out. Lay your sinamay flat on a table, place the template on the bias (diagonally across the weave) and pin it in place. Cut out the sinamay and repeat this seven times so you have seven petals.

2 Take your first sinamay petal, and starting on one of the curved sides of the petal shape, a couple of inches (5 cm) up from the point, fold over a tiny bit of sinamay – no more than about 2 mm. Holding the folded sinamay firmly between your finger and thumb, begin to roll the fold back and forth until you've got a nicely rolled edge. When I first started doing this it took me hours of practice to get it right, but I got there eventually. You may find it helpful to slightly dampen your fingers with water as this can help the fabric roll a little more easily. You'll know when it's working because you'll end up with a really tightly rolled edge and there won't be any stray fibres – if you've any got stray fibres showing you're not quite there yet – keep practising. Continue to roll the fabric all the way round the petal shape. You don't need to roll right up to the points as you're going to cut the points of the petals off later.

3 With the rolled edge on the outside, fold the petal over so that the two points meet. Secure the two ends together by sewing through with a needle and thread. Repeat this process for all seven petals.

4 Now gather the finished petals together in your hand, stems together, to create a flower. I do this by placing one petal in the middle and the others around it, but arrange them however you feel looks best. Tack the petals together through the stems with a needle and thread, making sure that each petal is securely attached to the others. Give them a shake to make sure they're secure. Put them to one side.

5 Now take four or five goose feathers and secure them together with a needle and matching thread, wrapping the thread around the base of the feathers a few times and stitching through them. Once they're secure, you may want to slightly curl them if you think they're too straight – it depends on the look you want to achieve. Experiment! You can curl feathers just as you would ribbon – carefully with the back of your scissors or a metal edge. Repeat until you have as many bundles of feathers as you want – I'm using eight for this fascinator.

6 Place the feather bundles between the petals and sew them in securely. You might want to put a dab of glue onto the ends of the feathers if you're worried about them coming loose. Give them all a gentle tug and shake to make sure they're secure.

3

4

5

6

7 Trim away any excess fabric at the bottom of the fascinator to give it a neat finish. Make very sure you cut below where you've stitched, otherwise it'll all fall apart, and you'll have to start again! I've done it myself and it's the most frustrating thing in the world – and it's such an easy mistake to make. I find it easier to cut little bits off one at a time rather than cutting through it all at once. Once cut, make sure it hasn't come loose (hold it tight and put a bit more thread in quickly if it has), and then flatten the petals a bit with the palm of your hand – just push them down gently.

8 Take your fascinator base and place the flower in the centre of it. Sew up through from the underside of the base into the stitching of the flower, all the way round until it's secure. This will take a lot of stitching. Do the obligatory shake and tug test – remember it's got to withstand all that the weather can throw at it. Now take each petal at a time and sew it down to the edge of the fascinator base. This does three things: it hides the join where the base of the flower is attached to the fascinator base, it flattens the fascinator to create a prettier flower shape, and it also makes the whole piece a lot more secure. Just take it slowly and methodically until all the petals are securely attached to the edge of the fascinator base. Next, I do what I call 'faffing about' with it – pulling the feathers into place between the petals and curling them until the fascinator looks exactly how I want it to look.

9 Finally, attach a comb to the base in the usual way – a couple of stitches through the fascinator base and around the teeth of the comb at each end, and you're done.

Sophie

Ideas to steal
Another example of a fascinator using this technique is Arianna. I have used smaller petals and decorated with hackle and cut coque feathers.

Arianna

FEATHER POM POM
INTERMEDIATE PROJECT NO. 2:
FLORENTINA

Approx 3 hours **Skill level** Intermediate

You will need: Approx ½ yard (½ m) of ostrich feathers; a 6 inch (15 cm) strip of coque feathers (or 8–10 individual feathers); 4–5 crystal stems; 1 yard (1 m) of matching ribbon; needle and matching thread; fabric scissors; hair band; floral tape; glue. Ostrich feathers can be bought on a fringe or can be taken directly from the spine of the feather. Whatever you choose you'll need to remove the feathers so that each feather is loose.

1 Make about 16 to 20 small bundles of ostrich feathers, approximately 20 or 30 feathers in each bundle (this is a rough guide – you can have more or less, you just don't want the bundles to be too thick as the feathers need to be secured together tightly – if they are too thick, the centre feathers will fall out).

2 Secure them together with a needle and thread by wrapping the thread around and stitching through the base of the bundle, then securing it tightly with a knot. You might like to put a dab of glue on the end of each bundle to give it a bit more security but you don't have to – as long as your stitching and knots are tight they should stay in place.

3 Now to build the mount. Start by securing a crystal stem in to one of the feather bundles, in the same way that you secured the end of the feather bundle – sewing around and through the stem and feathers. Now add more feather bundles to this first feather bundle, one at a time, as well as the coque feathers and remaining crystal stems. You may find it easier to work with the mount upside down. Always make sure it's secure at each stage, giving the feathers and stems a little tug. Carry on until you've used up all of your coque feathers, feather bundles and crystal stems. Fluff it all out till you're happy with the way it looks. Give it a shake to make sure it's secure.

4 Trim the bottom to neaten it, making very sure you're always cutting below your stitching.

5 Take your hair band and decide where you want the mount to be positioned on your head. I find it easier to put the hair band on my head and hold the mount in place. Using a mirror, once you're happy with it's position, use your thumb to mark the spot on the hair band and then attach it to the hair band with floral tape. Make sure you wrap the tape tightly so that it squashes the end of the mount closely in to the hair band. This will make it easier to cover with ribbon and it will won't look too bulky.

6 Dab a spot of glue onto the end of the metal hair band, and start winding your ribbon tightly round it. Keep going until you've covered the base of the mount in ribbon. When you get to the end of the feather mount base, all you've got to do is take the ribbon behind the feathers and carry on wrapping the ribbon around the hair band. Continue until you've wrapped the whole band in ribbon. Glue the end of the ribbon securely in place to finish it off.

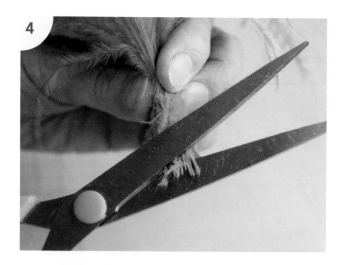

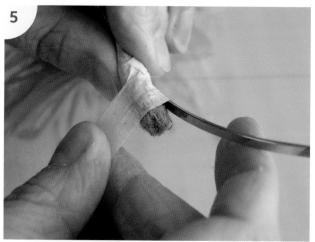

Florentina

Penelope

Stephanie

Florentina is basically a big feather pom-pom. A bit fun and a bit flirty, and it moves really nicely in the breeze. It makes me think of the fronds of a lovely plant wafting under the Mediterranean sea...

Other examples are **Penelope** which has a butterfly centre, and **Stephanie** which uses two-tone coloured ostrich feathers and is a really massive pom pom.

46

FEATHER MOUNT
INTERMEDIATE PROJECT NO. 3: ALICIA

Approx ½ a day   Skill level Intermediate

You will need: Approx ½ yard (½ m) hackle feathers. (you can buy hackle feathers either on a fringe or a fan – you need them loose for this project, so start by removing all the feathers); approx 5 diamond-trimmed coque feathers; 5–6 curled feather spines; 5–6 crystal stems; approx 6 inches (15 cm) craft wire; wire cutters; needle and matching thread; floral tape; matching satin ribbon; hair band; glue.

You might look at this project and wonder what's the difference between it and Florentina on page 44. Well, they are actually quite different fascinators. Florentina is basically a large pom pom – Alicia on the other hand is a mount, built using wire. The mount is created by attaching feathers all along a wire, which means the mount can be manipulated into whatever shape you like. It's a more versatile technique than Florentina and a great technique to have under your belt.

1 Take your craft wire and place a coque feather at the end, with the feather sticking out beyond the end of the wire, making sure there is enough overlap to secure it to the wire. Place around it some hackle feathers, curving outwards. Add some crystal stems in wherever you want them to appear (there are no rules about positioning here – it's all down to personal preference). Secure all this to the wire with a needle and double thread – wrapping the thread tightly around the feathers and crystal stems a few times. Secure the thread with a knot. If you want to use a bit of glue for extra piece of mind, feel free – just dab a bit on the wire before arranging the feathers and crystal stems around it.

2 Moving a little way down the wire, take a couple more coque feathers and crystal stems, and place them against the wire, attaching them in the same way as above. Continue to build up the mount in this way, moving down the wire, adding more and more feathers as you go. Use less feathers towards the end of the wire, so the mount has a nice balance of feathers, and leave 1 to 2 inches (2.5–5 cm) of wire exposed at the end. Once everything is secure, gently bend the wire to create a curve which sits snugly against your head.

3 Now to attach the mount to the hair band. Place the exposed wire end of the mount against the start of the hair band and wrap floral tape securely around both the mount and the hair band, until you get to the start of the feathers.

4 Next, dab a spot of glue onto the end of the hair band. Place the end of your matching ribbon over the glue and hold it tightly against the hair band.

5 Start wrapping the ribbon around the hair band.

6 When you get to the start of the feathers, take the ribbon behind the feathers and carry on wrapping the ribbon around the hair band all the way to the end.

7 And there you have it! Your first wire-mount fascinator.

Alicia

Making fascinators is pretty unique in the craft world, as you really don't need to buy a lot of the 'proper' equipment. I've used Sellotape instead of floral tape, woks and wooden fruit bowls instead of hat blocks, garden wire instead of millinery wire and CDs as templates. If you're going to spend money, spend it on good quality thread, feathers and fabrics. That's what you're ultimately going to be looking at after all.

Rose

50

SINAMAY CALLA LILIES
INTERMEDIATE PROJECT NO. 4: LILY

Approx 1 day **Skill level** Intermediate

You will need: Approx ½ yard (½ m) sinamay; approx ½ yard (½ m) goose feathers; 5 organza butterflies; 8 inches (20 cm) craft or millinery wire; wire cutters; a length of 0.4 mm jewellery wire; tape measure or ruler; fabric scissors; needle and matching thread; invisible thread; glass head pins; hair band; glue (optional).

1 We'll start this project by making the lilies. First lay your sinamay flat on your work top. Measure and cut out three squares: a 7 inch (18 cm) square, a 5 inch (12.5 cm) square, and a 4 inch (10 cm) square. Take the largest square and fold over one edge by approximately ½ inch (1 cm) and firmly press along the fold with your fingers to crease it. Turn the square through 90 degrees and fold over an adjacent edge. You should now have two folded edges next to each other and two free edges next to each other.

2 Fold the square in half to create a triangle so that the folded edges meet and the two free edges meet.

3 Pick the triangle up and hold it with the point facing you. Bend the two short sides of the triangle up together to create a cone shape, and tuck the unfolded edges inside the two folded edges, all the way along. Pin the join together. Using a stab stitch, sew all the way along the join with your needle and matching thread. When you have finished stitching, if there are any stray bits of sinamay sticking out just snip them off to neaten it up.

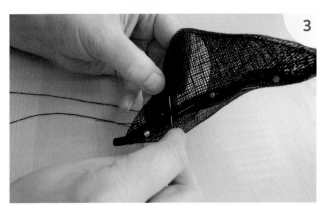

4 Now bend the open ends of the lily out, round and down to create a trumpet shape at the mouth. Repeat the steps above with the other two squares until you have three lilies, each one a little smaller than the other.

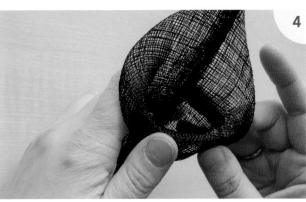

5 To make the feather spray, take four or five goose feathers and approximately 8 inches (20 cm) of craft wire. Dab a spot of glue around the end of the wire and place the cluster of feathers around the glue. Take your matching thread and wrap it around the feathers and the wire to secure the feathers in place. Tie the thread off and give it the obligatory shake test. There's no need to cut the thread at this stage because you can use it to secure the next group of feathers below this one.

6 Now dab a bit more glue around the wire about an inch (2.5 cm) below the first group of feathers. Take seven or eight feathers this time, and place them on to the wire where the glue, is in the same way as you attached the first group of feathers above. Repeat this process all the way down the wire, adding more feathers towards to the centre and less towards the end. Once you get to the end of the feather mount, either wrap a bit of floral tape around the bottom, or if you haven't got any floral tape, carry on wrapping your thread around to cover up all of the untidy bits and to secure the end of the mount. If you've used white floral tape you can just use a black marker pen to colour it, once it's wrapped in place. I've been known to raid my daughters' pencil case for felt tip pens before now!

7 Attach your butterfly to the end of a piece of jewellery wire, and then secure the other end of the wire, at the desired length, to the craft wire in between the feathers. Repeat with three or four butterflies so they look like they're just hovering around and within the feather spray.

8 Now to attach the feathers to the sinamay lilies. Place the base of the feather mount right inside the largest lily and, holding the craft wire against the back of the lily, sew through the lily and the feather mount from the back of the lily to secure the feathers in place. Sew all the way down the lily.

9 Now place the two smaller lilies side by side inside the top of the big lily containing the feather mount – this also has the advantage of covering up the base of the feather mount. Attach the small lilies to the large one in a couple of places – just stitch through the tops of the smaller lilies into the back of the larger lily using your black thread. You won't see the stitching as long as it's neat. You can also decorate the lilies with a couple of organza butterflies by sewing them in place wherever you want.

10 To attach the mount to your hair band, take a small 2 inch (5 cm) length of matching bias strip. Fold both ends over to neaten it up. Work out where the lily is going to sit on your head by playing with it in the mirror, and then sew one side of the bias strip on to the underside of the lily, making sure the long folded edge of the bias strip is facing forwards when you are wearing the lily. Sew all the way down the length of the bias strip so it's securely attached to the underside of the big lily. Then place the hair band inside the folded bias strip where you want it to go, dab some glue along it, and sew the top of the bias strip down over the hair band to secure it in place.

11 Mould the feather covered wire mount to curve round against the hair band so that it looks like the pictures over the page, and sew down some of the feathers to the hair band using invisible thread. You may get away with just sewing one in place – just do whatever is needed to make sure they are securely attached and so that the feather mount curves nicely around the hair band.

Lily

Ideas to steal

For *Bernadette*, I made contrasting coloured lilies and placed a smaller one inside each of the larger ones. I then trimmed it all with hackle feathers and attached it to a small sinamay disc.

Bernadette

WORKING WITH CRIN
INTERMEDIATE PROJECT NO. 5: MIA

Approx ½ a day   Skill level Intermediate

You will need: 1 yard (1 m) of 4 inch (10 cm) wide crin; 2 butterfly stems; needle and matching thread; matching fabric-covered hair band; fabric scissors.

Note: Crin is a very sensitive fabric – you've got to be very gentle with it. It's not like sinamay as it doesn't always do what it's told – you've got to keep playing with it until you get the 'look' you're after. BUT – and here's why it can be difficult to work with – the more you play with it the more the fibres will unravel.

If you'd like to learn more about working with crin, see our book on crin on the **how2hats.com** website.

1 Crin usually has a thread woven in to it along one edge. Start by making a knot in one end of this thread so that when you pull the thread from the other end it doesn't all come out. Take the thread at the other end and gently pull it. This will cause the crin to begin to gather together.

2 Continue pulling until all the crin is gathered together. Tie both ends of the thread together in a knot to stop the crin unravelling. Trim the ends of the thread (although I never like to cut off too much in case something goes wrong later).

3 Now take one of the free cut edges of the crin and gather and pinch it together. Gently twist it to create a 'stem' of crin.

4 Holding this 'stem' tightly between your finger and thumb, wrap your thread through and around it to secure it. Repeat this process with the other free cut edge of the crin.

5 Now holding both stems firmly with one hand, gather the rest of the crin together. Twist it, pinch it, gather it, manipulate it, play with it – whatever you need to do to make a nice shape. But bear in mind what I said earlier – crin 'deteriorates' the more you play with it – so it's a bit of a balancing act. Try not to overdo it.

6 When you're happy with the shape you've created, stitch through the base that you're holding tightly. You may find that you need to do this in stages – manipulating it a bit and then tacking it together, and then manipulating some more. It doesn't have to look exactly like the one in the picture – you just need to create something you're happy with. Let crin work it's mysterious magic!

7 Now take the butterfly stems and gently insert them into the centre of the crin swirl you've created. It's all down to preference as to where you want them to sit – mine sit about an inch above the centre of the swirl, partially hidden by the crin. Once you are happy with their position, secure them in place with a needle and thread. Trim away any excess crin underneath, and any excess wire from the butterflies, to leave a neat finish underneath. Make sure you trim below your stitches otherwise it'll all fall apart.

8 Now take your fabric-covered hair band and sew the crin onto the hair band using your needle and matching thread.

Mia

Ideas to steal
Emma (below) uses the same principle as **Mia**, but rather than creating a swirl, I've created a fan shape. I created the bow underneath by removing the thread from the edge of the crin and folding and pinching it in the centre.

Emma

SINAMAY DISC
INTERMEDIATE PROJECT NO. 6: HENRIETTA

Approx 1 day   **Skill level** Intermediate

You will need: 1 yard (1 m) sinamay; 3 burnt peacock eyes; spring wire; wire cutters; 2 yards (2 m) bias strip; a 3 inch (7.5 cm) fascinator base; fabric scissors; needle and matching thread; dressmaker's chalk or pencil; glass head pins; masking tape or floral tape; hair band; glue.

For the feather burning you will need: Household bleach; two small plastic bowls; rubber gloves; newspaper or an old tea towel; spoon or wooden spatulas (the sort you get in coffee shops – I always collect a few whenever I buy a coffee – my handbag always has some in it!)

Start by making a large fascinator base – approx 10 inches (25 cm) across. To do this, follow the instructions for the small fascinator base in the Basic Techniques (page 8), but just make it larger. To make your template, use anything in the house that is the right size – I drew round a casserole dish lid for mine.

Now use the left-over bias strip from making the base to create a double bow. See the instructions on page 24 for Colette. Put this to one side to use later.

For this project you will need to burn some feathers. This is a technique used to thin out feathers and to remove their natural colours, making them look more delicate. See the instructions over the page for how to do this.

1 Once your feathers are dried, arrange them how you'd like them on the fascinator base. Make sure that the join in the bias strip around the edge of the fascinator base is positioned so that it's at the back of your head and can't easily be seen. (You'll have to decide on which side of the head the fascinator is going to be worn before you know which is going to be the back of the fascinator).

2 When you are happy with the positioning of the feathers, sew them securely onto the sinamay disc with matching thread. Use the least amount of stitches possible to keep it neat, and insert your needle through the side of the spine rather than through the top. Do this at the bottom of the spine where the bow will cover the stitching, and again half way up, to secure them in place. I find it easier to start stitching half way up the feather, and then to stitch the bottom of the feather to the base – if you start stitching at the bottom, the feather tends to move around too much. Tie the thread off on the underside of the fascinator base. Now attach the other two feathers in the same way, where you want them to sit.

3 Take the sinamay bow you made earlier and place it over the bottom of the peacock feathers to cover the ends of the feathers and the stitching. Pin it in place and secure from behind with matching thread.

4 Work out where the fascinator is going to sit on your head by playing with it in the mirror. Take a small length of bias strip, open it out and fold over one end to neaten it and to stop it fraying. Then measure it across the small fascinator base, and cut it ½ inch (1 cm) longer than the base. Fold the other cut end over and you'll have a strip as wide as the fascinator base with both ends folded over. Take the hair band and slide it into the bias strip, pushing it right to the back, up against the long fold. Glue under the end flaps and then all along one inner edge of the bias strip, then close it around the hair band and squeeze tight. Sew the bias strip with the hair band to the underside of the small fascinator base using a stab stitch.

5 Now place the small fascinator base and hair band in the centre of the large disc, again making sure the join in the bias strip around the fascinator base is at the back when you wear it. Attach it to the large disc with matching thread using a stab stitch so that the thread won't be seen on the top of the fascinator.

FEATHER BURNING

When you burn feathers, they start out looking like **A**, and end up looking like **B**. As you can see, the burnt feather is a much more delicate and the colour has been bleached out of it.

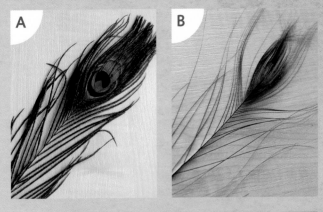

1 Put your rubber gloves on. Put clean water in one of your plastic tubs, and a small amount of bleach in your other plastic tub – just enough to cover the feathers. Place the feathers into the bleach. Gently swish them around in the bleach with your spoon or wooden spatula.

2 If you watch them carefully, you'll start to see bubbles forming around the feathers and the some of the small 'veins' will begin to drop off. The colour will also start to run, and the bleach will begin to look cloudy and muddy. All this only takes a minute or so.

3 When you see that only the main stem and the first set of side veins remain, move the feathers in to the tub containing clean water. If after washing the feather you think it needs a bit longer in the bleach, just repeat the process above until you're happy with the result.

4 Carefully comb out the feathers with your fingers and leave them to air-dry on your tea towel.

Note: Because feathers are natural products, each

time you work on them you'll get a different result – no two burnt feathers will look the same. This isn't a problem, but it does mean that it may be a bit of trial and error to get the effect you're after.

*H*enrietta

Ideas to steal
For Georgia, I used a layer of lace over the top of the sinamay and two turkey arrow quills. For Zeta I made a two-colour feather mount, and finished it with a double sinamay bow.

*Z*eta

*G*iorgia

65

Advanced projects

Now that you have learnt how to incorporate the basic techniques into specific projects, it's time to move on to the next level. These advanced projects are the perfect way to improve your skills and challenge yourself further, and the finished fascinators will add a significant 'wow factor' to any outfit.

Making these advanced fascinators is also a great opportunity to acquire some of the more specialist hat making tools like hat blocks. They may look expensive, but if treated well, they will last a lifetime. And it will increase the range of fascinators you can make if you build up a nice little collection.

WIRED SINAMAY
ADVANCED PROJECT NO. 1: STELLA

Approx 1 day   Skill level Advanced

You will need: 1 yard (1 m) sinamay; millinery wire; wire cutters; floral or masking tape; 2 yards (2 m) Petersham or cross-grain ribbon; 3 inch (7.5 cm) fascinator base; fabric scissors; large silk flower (available from many haberdashery shops or make one with the book from **how2hats.com**); needle and matching thread; dressmaker's chalk; glass head pins; hair band.

1 Lay out your sinamay and fold it in half to create a double layer. Depending on how good you are at drawing, either draw a freehand circle or draw around a circular object approximately 16 inches (40 cm) in diameter. Pin the two pieces together and cut the circle out.

2 Measure and cut a length of millinery wire to fit right around the circumference of your circle, plus a bit extra so you have enough to secure the ends together.

3 Create two loops at the ends of the wire by bending the wire back on itself. Link the two loops together and cover the join with a little floral or masking tape. Now take a needle and double matching thread and, using a blanket stitch, secure the wire to the edge of the sinamay all the way round. This is the same technique as for making a fascinator base (see page 8).

4 Take your Petersham or cross-grain ribbon and fold it in half along it's length. Iron the fold and place the fold over the edge of the disc so it covers the wire. Starting an inch (2.5 cm) or so in from the end, stab stitch the ribbon to the edge of the sinamay with your needle and matching thread. Continue stitching all the way round. Cut off any excess ribbon, leaving enough to tuck under the free edge. Fold the edge of the ribbon over to give a neat finish and sew securely down.

5 Draw a 6 inch (15 cm) circle in the centre of your large sinamay disc with dressmaker's chalk, and cut the circle out. Take care not to let the sinamay fray at the edge.

6 Take your needle and matching thread and stitch all round the edge of this hole with a running stitch, about ¼ inch (5 mm) in from the edge, having first secured the end of the thread to the sinamay so it doesn't pull out.

7 Once you have tacked all the way round, gently pull the thread, gathering the sinamay together. Don't pull too hard otherwise the thread may pull out from the edge of the sinamay. Keep pulling until the hole in the centre disappears and the sinamay is all gathered up.

8 Now pinch the fabric, making sure you have all the centre gathered together and secure it with a needle and matching thread. This can be tricky. It can look really messy too – that's why we add a flower to the middle later on, to hide all this mess. Make sure you have stitched through and secured every free edge in the centre – as long as you do this you can be confident the fascinator won't fall apart later on.

5 6

7 8

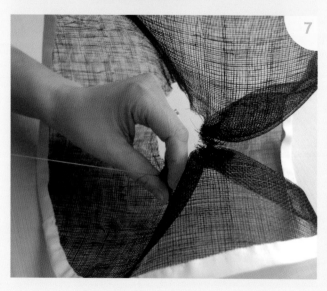

9 Taking the wired edge covered with the ribbon, gently bend the wire to create folds all round as in the picture below. Keep going until you have a nicely rippled edge all the way round.

10 When you are happy with the shape, we're going to hide the ugly join in the centre by trimming the fascinator with a large silk flower. It doesn't have to be a flower of course – it could be a brooch, a bow – anything that takes your fancy as long as it's big enough to cover the mess. Take your silk flower (or brooch or bow) and sew it to the centre

of the gathered fabric from behind. Now make a small matching fascinator base, 3 inches (7.5 cm) in diameter – see Basic Technique No. 2 (page 8). Trim the fascinator base in petersham ribbon rather than the usual sinamay, so that it matches the fascinator.

11 Turn the fascinator over and sew the small fascinator base into the centre using a stab stitch all the way round the edge. This will ensure the stitching does not show on the other side.

12 Attach the hair band to the base with a small length of bias strip – see step 4 on page 63 for how to do this.

9

10

11

12

Stella

Ideas to steal

Why not breathe new life into an old hat by removing the crown and rewiring the brim with millinery wire? You can then either make the wavy fan shape I've used for **Stella**, or get experimental and create your own unique style.

ADVANCED
PROJECT NO. 2
MIRABELLA

BLOCKED FASCINATOR
ADVANCED PROJECT NO. 2: MIRABELLA

Approx 2 days   Skill level Advanced

You will need: Hat block (I've used a small oval 'fez' style block from Guy Morse-Brown Hat Blocks: **www.hatblocks.co.uk**); 2 yards (2 m) sinamay; 8–10 marabou feathers; 6 x 3 mm pearls; spring wire; wire cutters; cling film (Saran wrap in the USA); plastic bowl; old tea towel; masking tape or floral tape; blocking pins; sinamay stiffener; needle and matching thread; invisible thread; fabric scissors; glass head pins; millinery elastic.

1   Take your small fascinator hat block, cover it in cling film (Saran wrap in the USA) and secure the cling film to the base of the block with masking tape. Measure across the hat block in both directions (i.e. up one side, across the top and down the other side) and add 4 inches (10 cm) to each measurement. This will then give you the dimensions for your sinamay. So if the block measures 8 x 8 inches (20 x 20 cm), then you need a double layer of sinamay 12 x 12 inches (30 x 30 cm). Or you can use a piece 12 x 24 inches (30 x 60 cm) and fold it in half.

2   Run your double layer of sinamay under the hot tap or soak it in hot water in your bowl until it is completely saturated.

3   You may want to place an old tea towel on your work surface to stop it getting too wet. Turn the block upside down so it's easier to work with, and place the block in the centre of the fabric. Holding the sinamay tightly against the hat block, start by pulling one corner of the sinamay square tightly over the bottom edge of the block. Pin this corner down to the underside of the block, near the edge, with a blocking pin. Now turn the block around and pull the opposite

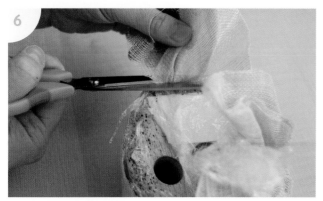

side of the square tightly over the base of the block and pin that down near the edge of the block.

4 Repeat this for the remaining two corners. Once all four quarters have been pinned down and the sinamay is secure, you can continue to pin the rest of the sinamay to the block. As you pull the sinamay round the edge of the bottom of the block little by little, you need to pull it in such a way as to get rid of as many of the wrinkles in the sinamay as possible. This can be hard on the hands and fingers, but it gets easier with practice.

5 Once all of the pins are in place and the fabric sits wrinkle-free and tightly against the block, stiffen the sinamay. If you're using undiluted sinamay stiffener, mix four parts water to one part sinamay stiffener (or use ready-mixed stiffener) and with a sponge, dab the stiffener all over the sinamay. Leave the block to dry overnight at room temperature. Once the sinamay is completely dry remove the pins.

6 While the sinamay is still on the block, cut the excess sinamay away, using the edge of the block as your guide. This should give you a straight neat finish all around.

7 Remove the sinamay from the block and cling film by gently prising it away with your fingers – take extra care not to stretch the sinamay or pull it out of shape. You then need to decide whether to cut the hat down – it's entirely down to personal preference. If you think it needs reducing in height a bit, I would always start by cutting off half an inch (1 cm) at a time until you are happy. For this project I've left it as it is as I quite like the depth.

8 To help the hat keeps its shape you need to wire the loose edge. Take your spring wire and measure around the base of the block. Cut the wire with wire cutters, leaving enough to overlap the ends a little. Secure the two ends together with either floral or masking tape. Now decide which is the front and which is the back of the fascinator – you always put the bit of the wire secured with floral tape at the back.

9 Using a blanket stitch and matching thread, sew the wire to the edge of the blocked fascinator. This doesn't need to be very neat as it's going to be hidden under a bias strip.

10 Take your piece of bias strip in matching sinamay. Starting where the tape on the wire is, and, leaving an inch (2.5 cm) of bias strip free, sew the bias strip over the wired edge of the hat with a stab stitch and matching thread. Sew all the way round to cover the wire and edge of the blocked fascinator. When you get to the end, cut off the excess bias strip, leaving enough to tuck under the inch you left free at the beginning. Sew both ends down.

11 Your hat should look like this – it's now ready to trim.

12 We'll start with the roses. To make a sinamay rose, draw and cut out the large rose paper pattern on page 89. It's basically a rectangle, 18 inches (45 cm) long by 4 inches (10 cm) wide, with a point and rounded corners at both ends. Pin the template to the sinamay on the bias (diagonally across the weave) and cut it out. Repeat this several times until you have enough flowers to trim your hat – on my fascinator I've used three large roses and three small roses. Fold the sinamay in half lengthways and press along the fold firmly with your fingers. (If you would like a sharper finish you can iron the fold. Be careful though, because sinamay cut on the bias is liable to stretch when ironed, so make sure you press and lift the iron rather than sliding it along the fabric).

9   10

11   12

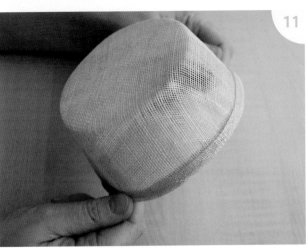
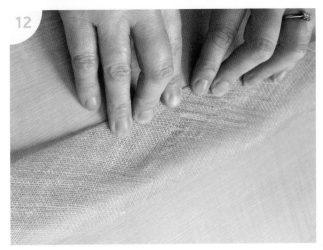

13 Take your needle and matching thread and secure one end of it to the sinamay. Using a tack stitch, sew the two raw edges together all the way along, about ¼ inch (5 mm) in from the edge. Leave the end of the thread loose – don't finish it off as you will be using the remaining thread to gather the fabric.

14 Now gently pull the thread through to gather the fabric, which should naturally fall into a spiral shape.

15 Release the thread and take hold of the point where you finished stitching.

16, 17 Now pinch, twist and gather – rolling the fabric to form the centre of a rose. You can make it as tight or as loose as you like. Make sure that the centre of the rose does not move upwards as you gather it, otherwise when you stitch through the bottom of the rose to secure it, the centre will not be secured and may work loose. Stitch through the bottom to secure

the rose in place – make sure your needle goes through all the sections of the rose. Continue to roll and stitch, and also incorporate some pleats if you like – a rose with lots of pleats will resemble an open flower, and one that is mainly rolled will be more like a bud. When you get to the end of the fabric, roll this over to create a neat finish and secure with a few stitches. Make two more large roses. Then make your three smaller roses – again see the pattern on page 89.

18 Now make three petals to act as leaves. See Courtney (pages 28–29) – the template is on page 89. Make them a little smaller than Courtney – mine are made from a half-circle template about 6 ½ inches (16 cm) in diameter. You can probably make them from off-cuts. I don't even measure them half the time now – I just cut them out by eye. Making fascinators is a very forgiving job! Figure 18 shows what they all look like – petal, small and large rose.

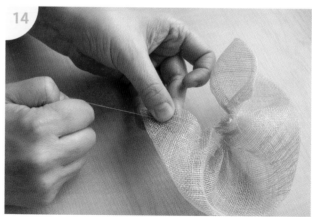

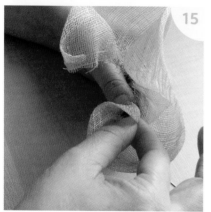

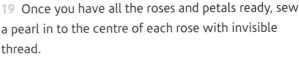

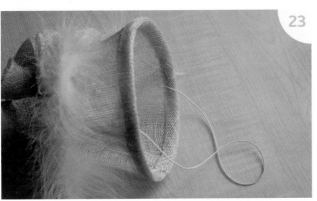

19 Once you have all the roses and petals ready, sew a pearl in to the centre of each rose with invisible thread.

20 Now to arrange the flowers and petals. I find it easier to make the bouquet in my hand to see how best to arrange them. Once you've got them arranged how you'd like, start by sewing the two centre flowers together. Then build up the bouquet by sewing the other flowers and petals to these two. This way you end up with a bouquet that you know is secure before you attach it to the blocked base.

21 Secure just the centre of the bouquet to the top of the blocked base, leaving space all around in which to feed the feathers. Add the feathers where you want them between the base of the bouquet and the top of the blocked base – whatever you think looks nice.

22 Stitch the feathers in from underneath the blocked base, making sure they are all secure. Now go round and sew through the blocked base, the flowers and leaves to secure them all down. Give it a good shake to make sure it's all secure.

23 Secure one end of a length of millinery elastic to one side of the blocked base. Place the fascinator on your head and stretch the elastic round to the other side until it's nice and snug on your head. Hold the loose end of the elastic in place with your finger, cut, tie a knot and sew it in. Voilà – your first blocked fascinator!

Ideas to steal

Daisy is a mini pill-box covered in fabric daisies, with a Swarovski crystal centre. I blocked this fascinator using a coffee jar lid! **Simone** is a pill-box trimmed with spotted veiling and a feather flower.

Mirabella

Daisy

Simone

YOUR PIÈCE DE RÉSISTANCE...
ADVANCED PROJECT NO. 3: CATHERINE

Approx **1 day**   Skill level **Advanced**

You will need: ½ yard (½ m) sinamay in one colour
(or off-cuts); approx 2 yards (2 m) bias strip in a
contrasting colour; 2 coque feather fans, about 10–12
inches (25–30 cm) long; 2 x 4 inch (10 cm) fascinator
bases; 7 x 8 mm pearls; needle and matching thread;
glass head pins; fabric scissors; cotton bias strip (only
required if you're making the coque fan yourself); hair
band; glue.

1 Start by making the flower centre. Follow steps 1–9
for Courtney (pages 28–29), but make six petals, not
five. Then take your needle and matching thread and
sew through the sides of the bases of all the petals
until you have all six petals on your thread. When you
pull the thread, you'll create the flower shape as shown
in the picture. Sew all the petals securely together.

2 Now take your bias strip. Hold the strip flat between
your thumb and finger and start to create a large figure
of eight loop.

3 Continue until you have six large loops (i.e. three
figures of eight) all sitting on top of one another.
Check they are the right size by placing your sinamay
flower in the middle – the loops should stick out
beyond the flower. (You can make the loops all in one
go, with one length of bias strip, or, if you find it easier,
create three individual figure of eight loops and secure
them all together with a needle and thread).

4 If you have made the six loops from one continuous
strip, secure the loops by stitching through the centre.
You'll see that I'm using yellow thread on purple bias,
but that doesn't matter as the stitching is not going
to be seen when it's behind the flower. Trim away the
excess bias strip to neaten it up.

5 Place the flower in the centre of the bias strip loops, so that each petal sits within a loop. The curves of the loops need to face towards you. Sew the flower and the bias strips together in the centre, then give it a shake to make sure it's all secure.

6 Take one of your fascinator bases (see Basic Technique No. 2, page 8). Turn it upside down and place your two coque fans inside the base so that they make a circle of feathers. Pin them in place and then sew the fans to the fascinator base using a stab stitch. The feathers should form a complete circle – if there are any gaps, you can manipulate individual feathers by sewing them down to the fascinator base where you want them to sit.

7 Take the flower and loops and sew your 8 mm pearls in to the centre of the flower with invisible thread. This will cover the join at the centre of the flower. Sew through each pearl a couple of times to make sure they're really securely attached. Sewing through them a couple of times also makes them sit flatter on the flower. Now place the joined flower and loops in the fascinator base to which you've just sewn the feather fans. The feathers need to sit between base of the flower and loops and the fascinator base, so you can't see into the middle of the fascinator base where all the stitching is. Sew through the flower petals in to the edge of the fascinator base all round.

8 Decide where you want the fascinator to sit on your head and where you want the feathers to sit. Then take your second fascinator base, and pin it to the base of the other fascinator base with just a couple of pins. Now this bit sounds complicated but it's really very simple. You've now got two fascinator bases sitting on top of each other at the base of your fascinator. You can now bend the fascinator base you've just pinned to the existing base out on one side, so that it will sit snugly on your head the right way. As you can see from the photo, the base of your fascinator now looks a bit like an open clam shell.

9   Now sew round where the 2 bases touch, so that the second fascinator base is securely attached to the first.

10   Take a 2 inch (5 cm) strip of matching bias strip and attach the fascinator to the hair band. For instructions on how to do this, see step 4 on page 63.

As an alternative to buying coque feather fans, you can make them yourself if you prefer.

Here's how you do it. Take two pieces of cotton bias. Each should be 1 ½ inches (3 cm) wide and 2 inches (5 cm) long. Taking approximately 20 coque feathers, glue the stems to one side of the fabric leaving a couple of millimetres gap between each feather. Once all of the feathers are glued down, take your other piece of fabric and place it on top of the feathers and fabric strip.

Now bend the fabric to create a semi circle shape; this will allow the feathers to spread out.

Sew through the two strips of cotton and feathers to secure them all in place. You might want to use a sewing machine for this, but you can sew it by hand if you prefer.

Repeat this process again to create a second fan.

I really hope you've enjoyed making the fascinators in this book. Have fun experimenting!

Catherine

Catherine is a real stand-out-from-the crowd piece. The perfect fascinator for a day at the races!

 # $\mathcal{P}$atterns

These patterns are displayed at half their correct size – just photocopy this page and enlarge it so they are double the size shown here.

COURTNEY & CATHERINE PETAL

3 INCH FASCINATOR BASE

MIRABELLA PETAL

MIRABELLA LARGE ROSE

SOPHIE PETAL

MIRABELLA SMALL ROSE

4 INCH FASCINATOR BASE

Suppliers

United Kingdom

General millinery supplies

Baxter Hart & Abraham:	www.baxterhart.co.uk
Parkin Fabrics:	www.parkinfabrics.co.uk
The Trimming Company:	www.thetrimmingcompany.com
Milliner Warehouse:	www.millinerwarehouse.co.uk

Feathers:

LBF Trade Ltd:	www.lbftrade.com
RuiTong Ltd:	www.ruitongltd.com
Jaffé et Fils Ltd:	www.jaffefeathers.co.uk

USA

General millinery supplies

Judith M:	www.judithm.com
Hats by Leko:	www.hatsupply.com

Feathers:

The Feather Place:	www.featherplace.com
Dersh Feathers:	www.dershfeather.com

Australia

Torb & Reiner:	www.torbandreiner.com
Feathers Online:	www.feathersonline.com.au
House of Adorn:	www.houseofadorn.com

Europe

De Vroey (Belgium):	www.devroeyhats.be
Hoedendingen (Netherlands):	www.hoedendingen.nl
Fratelli Reali (Italy):	www.fratellireali.it
Kopka (Germany:	www.kopka.de

For more suppliers, see our suppliers page on the how2hats.com website.

cknowledgements

This book could only have been written with the help of many people.

My friends and family who have supported me every step of the way – thank you from the bottom of my heart – you know who you are.

Bethune, whose enthusiasm and passion got me hooked on the wonderful craft of millinery from day one.

John my editor and publisher for his belief in me, faultless eye for detail, and for keeping me focused every step of the way.

Donna, John, Nigel and Ioana for their beautiful photography.

My sister Michelle, niece Courtney and Simone for their fabulous modelling of my creations.

My mother Lorraine for her unconditional love, encouragement and unwavering support, without whom none of this would have been possible.

Craig my husband, who never lost confidence in me, even when I doubted myself, and for enduring the endless hours I put into my work.

Finally to my beautiful children Olivia and Max, this is for you. I love you with all of my heart. xxx